S0-ACD-606

Place do I it

hots

and

Lots

and

Lots

Happy Anniversary

Bill

How Do I Love Thee?

HOW DO I LOVE THEE?

Beautiful Love Poems of Yesterday and Today
Selected by Linda Rhodes
Illustrated by David Johnson

HALLMARK EDITIONS

CONTENTS

'How Do I Love Thee?'

HOW DO I LOVE THEE?

How do I love thee? Let me count the ways.
I love thee to the depth and breadth and height
My soul can reach, when feeling out of sight
For the ends of Being and ideal Grace.
I love thee to the level of every day's
Most quiet need, by sun and candle-light.
I love thee freely, as men strive for Right;
I love thee purely, as they turn from Praise.
I love thee with the passion put to use
In my old griefs, and with my childhood's faith.
I love thee with a love I seemed to lose
With my lost saints—I love thee with the breath,
Smiles, tears, of all my life!—and, if God choose,
I shall but love thee better after death.

Elizabeth Barrett Browning

INTOXICATION

Neath a willow with ivy entangled
We take cover in blustery weather.
My arms are wreathed about you;
In my raincape we huddle together.

I was wrong: Not ivy, my dearest,
But hops encircle this willow.
Well, then, let's spread in its shelter
My cape for a rug and a pillow!

Boris Pasternak

SONG

O, it was out by Donnycarney,
When the bat flew from tree to tree,
My love and I did walk together,
And sweet were the words she said to me.

Along with us the summer wind
Went murmuring--O, happily!--
But softer than the breath of summer
Was the kiss she gave to me.

James Joyce

TO HIS COY MISTRESS

Had we but world enough, and time,
This coyness, Lady, were no crime.
We would sit down, and think which way
To walk, and pass our long love's day.
Thou by the Indian Ganges' side
Should'st rubies find: I by the tide
Of Humber would complain. I would
Love you ten years before the Flood:
And you should, if you please, refuse
Till the conversion of the Jews.
My vegetable love should grow
Vaster than empires, and more slow.
An hundred years should go to praise
Thine eyes, and on thy forehead gaze.
Two hundred to adore each breast:
But thirty thousand to the rest.
An age at least to every part,
And the last age should show your heart.
For Lady, you deserve this state;
Nor would I love at lower rate.

But at my back I always hear
Time's winged chariot hurrying near:
And yonder all before us lie
Deserts of vast eternity.

Thy beauty shall no more be found;
Nor, in thy marble vault, shall sound
My echoing song: then worms shall try
That long preserved virginity:
And your quaint honor turn to dust;
And into ashes all my lust.
The grave's a fine and private place,
But none, I think, do there embrace.

Now therefore, while the youthful hue
Sits on thy skin like morning dew,
And while thy willing soul transpires
At every pore with instant fires,
Now let us sport us while we may;
And now, like amorous birds of prey,
Rather at once our time devour,
Than languish in his slow-chapped power.
Let us roll all our strength, and all
Our sweetness, up into one ball:
And tear our pleasures with rough strife
Through the iron gates of life.
Thus, though we cannot make our sun
Stand still, yet we will make him run.

Andrew Marvell

COME NIGHT, COME ROMEO

Come night; come, Romeo; come, thou day in night;
For thou wilt lie upon the wings of night
Whiter than new snow on a raven's back.—
Come, gentle night,—come, loving, black-brow'd night,
Give me my Romeo; and, when he shall die,
Take him and cut him out in little stars,
And he will make the face of heaven so fine,
That all the world will be in love with night,
And pay no worship to the garish sun.—
O, I have bought the mansion of a love,
But not possest it; and, though I am sold,
Not yet enjoy'd: so tedious is this day,
As is the night before some festival
To an impatient child that hath new robes
And may not wear them.

William Shakespeare

From GO LITTLE, MY TRAGEDY

Memory of young and living nakedness:
O when I was twenty and in love,
Doped by day and half the night sleepless,
Doomed and saved and dazed and waked by love:
And, of course, moneyless for love and houseless,
Sure that earlier passions had not been love,
Swept back and forth from tenderness to madness
To eat and breathe and think my love, my love—
Not to possess her each day: not to possess
Her surety and fidelity as proved,
And every hour I could not see her, guess
A hundred men might see her and be moved.
At thirty, I wonder for a moment where
She is, how gold is all that golden hair.

Winfield Townley Scott

FOR MIRIAM

Do I not deal with angels
When her lips I touch

So gentle, so warm and sweet—falsity
Has no sight of her
O the world is a place of veils and roses
When she is there

I am come to her wonder
Like a boy finding a star in a haymow
And there is nothing cruel or mad or evil
Anywhere

Kenneth Patchen

SHE WALKS IN BEAUTY

She walks in beauty, like the night
   Of cloudless climes and starry skies;
And all that's best of dark and bright
   Meet in her aspect and her eyes:
Thus mellowed to that tender light
   Which heaven to gaudy day denies

One shade the more, one ray the less,
   Had half impaired the nameless grace
Which waves in every raven tress,
   Or softly lightens o'er her face;
Where thoughts serenely sweet express
   How pure, how dear, their dwelling-place.

And on that cheek, and o'er that brow,
   So soft, so calm, yet eloquent,
The smiles that win, the tints that glow,
   But tell of days in goodness spent,
A mind at peace with all below,
   A heart whose love is innocent!

George Gordon, Lord Byron

MY LOVE COMES WALKING

My love comes walking,
And these flowers
That never saw her til this day
Look up; but then
Bend down straightway.

My love sees nothing here but me,
Who never trembled thus before;
And glances down
Lest I do more.

My love is laughing;
Those wild things
Were never tame until I too,
Down-dropping, kissed
Her silvery shoe.

                    Mark Van Doren

A DECADE

When you came, you were like red wine and honey,
And the taste of you burnt my mouth with its sweetness.
Now you are like morning bread,
Smooth and pleasant.
I hardly taste you at all, for I know your savor;
But I am completely nourished.

Amy Lowell

THE LITTLE TOIL OF LOVE

I had no time to hate, because
The grave would hinder me,
And life was not so ample I
Could finish enmity.

Nor had I time to love; but since
Some industry must be,
The little toil of love, I thought,
Was large enough for me.

                    Emily Dickinson

THE PASSIONATE SHEPHERD
TO HIS LOVE

Come live with me and be my love,
And we will all the pleasures prove
That hills and valleys, dales and fields,
Or woods or steepy mountain yields.

And we will sit upon the rocks,
And see the shepherds feed their flocks
By shallow rivers, to whose falls
Melodious birds sing madrigals.

And I will make thee beds of roses
And a thousand fragrant posies;
A cap of flowers, and a kirtle
Embroider'd all with leaves of myrtle.

A gown made of the finest wool
Which from our pretty lambs we pull;
Fair-lined slippers for the cold,
With buckles of the purest gold.

A belt of straw and ivy-buds
With coral clasps and amber studs:
And if these pleasures may thee move,
Come live with me and be my love.

                                   Christopher Marlowe

SHALL I COMPARE THEE
TO A SUMMER'S DAY?

Shall I compare thee to a summer's day?
Thou art more lovely and more temperate.
Rough winds do shake the darling buds of May,
And summer's lease hath all too short a date:
Sometime too hot the eye of heaven shines,
And often is his gold complexion dimm'd;
And every fair from fair sometime declines,
By chance or nature's changing course untrimm'd;
But thy eternal summer shall not fade,
Nor lose possession of that fair thou owest;
Nor shall Death brag thou wander'st in his shade,
When in eternal lines to time thou grow'st.
So long as men can breathe, or eyes can see,
So long lives this, and this gives life to thee.

William Shakespeare

'Love is . . .
A Rain of Diamonds in the Mind'

LOVE IS

a rain of diamonds
in the mind

the soul's fruit
sliced in two

a dark spring
loosed at the lips of light

under-earth waters
unlocked from their lurking
to sparkle in a crevice
parted by the sun

a temple
not of stone but cloud
beyond the heart's roar
and all violence

outside the anvil-stunned domain
unfrenzied space

between the grains of change
blue permanence

one short step
to the good ground

the bite into bread again

May Swenson

From TRUE LOVE

True Love is but a humble, low-born thing,
And hath its food served up in earthen ware;
It is a thing to walk with, hand in hand,
Through the everydayness of this work-day world
Baring its tender feet to every flint,
Yet letting not one heart-beat go astray
From Beauty's law of plainness and content;
A simple, fireside thing, whose quiet smile
Can warm earth's poorest hovel to a home....
Such is true Love, which steals into the heart
With feet as silent as the lightsome dawn
That kisses smooth the rough brows of the dark,
And hath its will through blissful gentleness,
Not like a rocket, which, with passionate glare,
Whirs suddenly up, then bursts, and leaves the night
Painfully quivering on the dazed eyes;
A love that gives and takes, that seeth faults
Not with flaw-seeking eyes like needle points,
But loving-kindly ever looks them down
With the o'ercoming faith that still forgives;
A love that shall be new and fresh each hour,
As is the sunset's golden mystery,
Or the sweet coming of the evening-star,
Alike, and yet most unlike, every day,
And seeming ever best and fairest now....

James Russell Lowell

MY FAMILIAR DREAM

I often dream strange penetrating dreams
Of one whom I adore and who loves me,
Whose image changes yet unchanging seems,
Who loves me well and understandingly.
No darkness is there in my heart for her:
For her alone its secrets all are plain:
She cools my pale moist forehead, while her prayer
Restores me, and her tears console my pain.
And is she fair or dark? I do not know.
Her name: 'Tis musical, recalling those
Of loved ones whom Life exiled long ago.
Her gaze is like a statue's, and her voice
—Her voice is grave and calm and is withdrawn,
Like those of dear ones gone beyond the bourne.

Paul Verlaine

LOVE-SONG

How shall I hold my soul, that it may not
be touching yours? How shall I lift it then
above you to where other things are waiting?
Ah, gladly would I lodge it, all-forgot,
with some lost thing the dark is isolating
on some remote and silent spot that, when
your depths vibrate, is not itself vibrating.
You and me—all that lights upon us, though,
brings us together like a fiddle-bow
drawing *one* voice from two strings it glides along.
Across what instrument have we been spanned?
And what violinist holds us in his hand?
O sweetest song.

Rainer Maria Rilke

MY DELIGHT AND THY DELIGHT

My delight and thy delight
Walking, like two angels white,
In the gardens of the night:

My desire and thy desire
Twining to a tongue of fire,
Leaping live, and laughing higher:

Thro' the everlasting strife
In the mystery of life.
Love, from whom the world begun,
Hath the secret of the sun.

Love can tell, and love alone,
Whence the million stars were strewn,
Why each atom knows its own,
How, in spite of woe and death,
Gay is life, and sweet is breath:

This he taught us, this we knew,
Happy is his science true,
Hand in hand as we stood
'Neath the shadows of the wood,
Heart to heart as we lay
In the dawning of the day.

                              Robert Bridges

A RED, RED ROSE

O, my luve is like a red, red rose,
That's newly sprung in June:
O, my luve is like the melodie
That's sweetly played in tune.

As fair art thou, my bonnie lass,
So deep in luve am I;
And I will luve thee still, my dear,
Till a' the seas gang dry.

Till a' the seas gang dry, my dear,
And the rocks melt wi' the sun;
And I will luve thee still, my dear,
While the sands o' life shall run.

And fare thee well, my only luve!
And fare thee well awhile!
And I will come again, my luve,
Tho' it were ten thousand mile!

Robert Burns

MY HEART
HAS ITS LOVE

The sea has its pearls,
The heaven its stars—
But my heart, my heart,
My heart has its love!

Heinrich Heine

RAIN

I have always hated the rain,
And the gloom of grayed skies.
But now I think I must always cherish
Rain-hung leaf and the misty river;
And the friendly screen of dripping green
Where eager kisses were shyly given
And your pipe-smoke made clouds
        in our damp, close heaven.

The curious laggard passed us by,
His wet shoes soughed on the shining walk.
And that afternoon was filled with a blurred glory—
That afternoon, when we first talked as lovers.

                                        Jean Starr Untermeyer

'To Reach My Dreamer's Paradise'

LOVERS' WINE

How dazzling are the heavens to-day!
Without bridle, bit or spurs, away!
Let's leave, on a steed of soaring wine,
For a faery realm and skies divine!

Oh like two angels tortured by
A pitiless fever let us fly
And the beckoning far mirage pursue
That glitters in morning's crystal blue!

Softly swaying on the wing
Of fancy's whirlwind we shall ride,
In a twin delirium glorying
And racing on, love, side by side;
So, tireless, truceless, we shall rise,
To reach my dreamer's paradise!

Charles Baudelaire

AN IMMORALITY

Sing we for love and idleness,
Naught else is worth the having.

Though I have been in many a land,
There is naught else in living.

And I would rather have my sweet,
Though rose-leaves die of grieving,

Than do high deeds in Hungary
To pass all men's believing.

Ezra Pound

SHE WAS A PHANTOM OF DELIGHT

She was a phantom of delight
When first she gleamed upon my sight;
A lovely apparition, sent
To be a moment's ornament;
Her eyes as stars of twilight fair;
Like twilight's, too, her dusky hair;
But all things else about her drawn;
A dancing shape, an image gay,
To haunt, to startle, and waylay.

I saw her upon nearer view,
A spirit, yet a woman too!
Her household motions light and free,
And steps of virgin-liberty;
A countenance in which did meet
Sweet records, promises as sweet;
A creature not too bright or good
For human nature's daily food;
For transient sorrows, simple wiles,
Praise, blame, love, kisses, tears, and smiles.

And now I see with eye serene
The very pulse of the machine;
A being breathing thoughtful breath,
A traveller between life and death;

The reason firm, the temperate will,
Endurance, foresight, strength, and skill;
A perfect woman, nobly planned,
To warm, to comfort, and command;
And yet a spirit still, and bright
With something of angelic light.

William Wordsworth

MEETING AT NIGHT

The grey sea and the long black land;
And the yellow half-moon large and low;
And the startled little waves that leap
In fiery ringlets from their sleep,
As I gain the cove with pushing prow,
And quench its speed i' the slushy sand.

Then a mile of warm sea-scented beach;
Three fields to cross till a farm appears;
A tap at the pane, the quick sharp scratch
And blue spurt of a lighted match,
And a voice less loud, through its joys and fears,
Than the two hearts beating each to each!

Robert Browning

BROWN PENNY

I whispered, "I am too young."
And then, "I am old enough";
Wherefore I threw a penny
To find out if I might love.
"Go and love, go and love, young man,
If the lady be young and fair."
Ah, penny, brown penny, brown penny,
I am looped in the loops of her hair.
O love is the crooked thing,
There is nobody wise enough
To find out all that is in it,
For he would be thinking of love
Till the stars had run away,
And the shadows eaten the moon.
Ah, penny, brown penny, brown penny,
One cannot begin it too soon.

William Butler Yeats

LUCK

Sometimes a crumb falls
From the tables of joy,
Sometimes a bone
Is flung.

To some people
Love is given,
To others
Only heaven.

Langston Hughes

GIFTS

1|28|13

I gave my first love laughter,
I gave my second tears,
I gave my third love silence
  Through all the years.

My first love gave me singing,
  My second eyes to see,
But oh, it was my third love
  Who gave my soul to me.

                    Sara Teasdale

WHEN I WAS ONE-AND-TWENTY

When I was one-and-twenty
    I heard a wise man say,
"Give crowns and pounds and guineas
    But not your heart away;
Give pearls away and rubies
    But keep your fancy free."
But I was one-and-twenty,
    No use to talk to me.

When I was one-and-twenty
    I heard him say again,
"The heart out of the bosom
    Was never given in vain;
'Tis paid with sighs aplenty
    And sold for endless rue."
And I am two-and-twenty,
    And oh, 'tis true, 'tis true.

A. E. Housman

'If Ever Two Were One,
Then Surely We'

LOVE SONG

Had I concealed my love
And you so loved me longer,
Since all the wise reprove
Confession of that hunger
In any human creature,
It had not been my nature.

I could not so insult
The beauty of that spirit
Who like a thunderbolt
Has broken me, or near it;
To love I have been candid,
Honest, and open-handed.

Although I love you well
And shall for ever love you,
I set that archangel
The depths of heaven above you;
And I shall lose you, keeping
His word, and no more weeping.

Elinor Wylie

TO MY DEAR AND LOVING HUSBAND

If ever two were one, then surely we.
If ever man were lov'd by wife, then thee.
If ever wife was happy in a man,
Compare with me, ye women, if you can.
I prize thy love more than whole mines of gold,
Of all the riches that the East doth hold.
My love is such that rivers cannot quench,
Nor ought but love from thee give recompense.
Thy love is such I can no way repay;
The heavens reward thee manifold I pray.
Then while we live, in love let's so persevere,
That when we live no more, we may live ever.

Anne Bradstreet

MEN MARRY WHAT THEY NEED.
I MARRY YOU

Men marry what they need. I marry you, morning by
morning, day by day, night by night, and every
marriage makes this marriage new.

In the broken name of heaven, in the light that
shatters granite, by the spitting shore, in air
that leaps and wobbles like a kite,

I marry you from time and a great door is shut and
stays shut against wind, sea, stone, sunburst, and
heavenfall. And home once more

inside our walls of skin and struts of bone,
man-woman, woman-man, and each the other, I marry
you by all dark and all dawn

and learn to let time spend. Why should I bother
the flies about me? Let them buzz and do. Men
marry their queen, their daughter, or their mother

by names they prove, but that thin buzz whines
through: when reason falls to reasons, cause is
true. Men marry what they need. I marry you.

John Ciardi

I WISH I COULD REMEMBER
THAT FIRST DAY

I wish I could remember that first day,
First hour, first moment of your meeting me,
If bright or dim the season, it might be
Summer or winter for aught I can say;
So unrecorded did it slip away,
So blind was I to see and to foresee,
So dull to mark the budding of my tree
That would not blossom yet for many a May.
If only I could recollect it, such
A day of days! I let it come and go
As traceless as a thaw of bygone snow;
It seemed to mean so little, meant so much;
If only now I could recall that touch,
First touch of hand in hand—did one but know!

Christina Rossetti

LOVE SONG

Sweep the house clean,
hang fresh curtains
in the windows
put on a new dress
and come with me!

The elm is scattering
its little loaves
of sweet smells
from a white sky!

Who shall hear of us
in the time to come?
Let him say there was
a burst of fragrance
from black branches.
William Carlos Williams

POEM IN PROSE

This poem is for my wife
I have made it plainly and honestly
The mark is on it
Like the burl on the knife

I have not made it for praise
She has no more need for praise
Than summer has
On the bright days

In all that becomes a woman
Her words and her ways are beautiful
Love's lovely duty
The well-swept room

Wherever she is there is sun
And time and a sweet air
Peace is there
Work done

There are always curtains and flowers
And candles and baked bread
And a cloth spread
And a clean house

Her voice when she sings is a voice
At dawn by a freshening sea
Where the wave leaps in the
Wind and rejoices

Wherever she is it is now
It is here where the apples are
Here in the stars
In the quick hour

The greatest and richest good—
My own life to live—
This she has given me

If giver could

Archibald MacLeish

WHEN YOU ARE OLD

When you are old and gray and full of sleep,
And nodding by the fire, take down this book,
And slowly read, and dream of the soft look
Your eyes had once, and of their shadows deep;

How many loved your moments of glad grace,
And loved your beauty with love false or true;
But one man loved the pilgrim soul in you,
And loved the sorrows of your changing face.

And bending down beside the glowing bars
Murmur, a little sadly, how love fled
And paced upon the mountains overhead
And hid his face amid a crowd of stars.

                                    William Butler Yeats

JENNY KISS'D ME

Jenny kiss'd me when we met,
    Jumping from the chair she sat in;
Time, you thief, who love to get
    Sweets into your list, put that in!
Say I'm weary, say I'm sad,
    Say that health and wealth have miss'd me,
Say I'm growing old, but add,
    Jenny kiss'd me.

Leigh Hunt

BELIEVE ME, IF ALL THOSE ENDEARING YOUNG CHARMS

Believe me, if all those endearing young charms,
Which I gaze on so fondly to-day,
Were to change by to-morrow, and fleet in my arms,
Like fairy-gifts fading away,
Thou wouldst still be adored, as this moment thou art,
Let thy loveliness fade as it will,
And around the dear ruin each wish of my heart
Would entwine itself verdantly still.

It is not while beauty and youth are thine own,
And thy cheeks unprofaned by a tear,
That the fervor and faith of a soul may be known,
To which time will but make thee more dear!
No, the heart that has truly loved never forgets,
But as truly loves on to the close,
As the sunflower turns to her god when he sets
The same look which she turned when he rose!

Thomas Moore

LET ME NOT TO THE MARRIAGE
OF TRUE MINDS

Let me not to the marriage of true minds
Admit impediments. Love is not love
Which alters when it alteration finds,
Or bends with the remover to remove:
O, no! it is an ever-fixed mark,
That looks on tempests and is never shaken;
It is the star to every wand'ring bark,
Whose worth's unknown, although his height be taken.
Love's not Time's fool, though rosy lips and cheeks
Within his bending sickle's compass come;
Love alters not with his brief hours and weeks,
But bears it out even to the edge of doom: —
If this be error and upon me proved,
I never writ, nor no man ever loved.

William Shakespeare

HOW MANY TIMES
DO I LOVE THEE?

How many times do I love thee, dear?
Tell me how many thoughts there be
   In the atmosphere
   Of a new-fall'n year,
Whose white and sable hours appear
The latest flake of Eternity: —
So many times do I love thee, dear.

How many times do I love again?
Tell me how many beads there are
   In a silver chain
   Of evening rain,
Unravelled from the tumbling main
And threading the eye of a yellow star:
So many times do I love again.

                   Thomas Lovell Beddoes

Printed on Hallmark Eggshell Book paper.
Set in Romanee, a 20th century typeface designed
by Jan van Krimpen of Holland. Romanee was
created to accompany the only surviving italic of
the 17th century typefounder Christoffel Van Dijck.
Designed by William M. Gilmore